Keeping Unusual Pets

GECKOS

Sonia Hernandez-Divers

Heinemann Library
Chicago, Illinois

© 2003 Reed Educational & Professional Publishing
Published by Heinemann Library,
an imprint of Reed Educational & Professional Publishing,
Chicago, Illinois

Customer Service 888-454-2279
Visit our website at www.heinemannlibrary.com

Designed by Celia Floyd
Originated by Dot Gradations Limited
Printed in China by WKT

07 06 05
10 9 8 7 6 5

Library of Congress Cataloging-in-Publication Data
Hernandez-Divers, Sonia, 1969-
 Geckos / Sonia Hernandez-Divers.
     p. cm. -- (Keeping unusual pets)
Includes bibliographical references (p.   ).
 ISBN 1-40340-282-5
 1. Geckos as pets--Juvenile literature. [1. Geckos as pets. 2. Pets.]
I. Title. II. Series.
 SF459.G35 H47 2002
 639.3'952--dc21
                    2002003163

Acknowledgments
The author and publishers are grateful to the following for permission to reproduce copyright material:
pp. 4, 33 (top) Bruce Coleman Collection/Animal Ark; p. 5 (left) Oxford Scientific Films/Zig Leszczynski; p. 5 (right) FLPA/Martin B. Withers; p. 6 (bottom) NHPA/Hello & Van Ingen; p. 7 Corbis/Joe McDonald; pp. 8, 10 (pic 2), 10 (pic 3) NHPA/Daniel Heuclin; p. 9 (top) Ardea/P. Morris; p. 9 (bottom) Oxford Scientific Films/Mike Linley; p. 10 (top) Oxford Scientific Films/Joe McDonald; pp. 10 (bottom), 12 Oxford Scientific Films/Michael Leach; p. 11 Ardea/Geoff Trinder; pp. 13 (left), 13 (right), 16, 17, 18, 19, 20, 21 (top), 21 (center), 21 (bottom), 22, 24, 25 (top), 25 (bottom), 26 (top), 26 (bottom), 27, 28, 30, 31 (bottom), 32, 34 (top), 34 (bottom), 35, 37 (top), 37 (bottom), 38, 39 (top), 43 (top), 43 (bottom), 44 (top) Gareth Boden Photography; pp. 14, 39 (bottom) Sonia M. Hernandez-Divers; p. 15 (top) FLPA; pp. 15 (bottom), 33 (bottom) NHPA/Image Quest 3-D; pp. 23, 29 (bottom), 36, 40, 41, 42, 44 (bottom) Tudor Photography; p. 29 (top) Ardea; p. 31 (top) Science Photo Library.

Cover photograph reproduced with permission of NHPA/Martin Harvey.

Some words are shown in bold, **like this.** You can find out what they mean by looking in the glossary.

No animals were harmed during the process of taking photographs for this series.

Contents

What Is a Gecko?

Geckos are beautiful and interesting animals. They are great fun to watch and are unlike any other pet you are likely to meet. Geckos are a type of lizard, and lizards belong to a large group of animals called **reptiles.** Like other reptiles, geckos have no hair and their bodies are covered with scales. They do not make milk for their young and they are **cold-blooded,** which means they need to soak up heat from their surroundings.

This is a typical lizard. It has scaly skin, a narrow head, and a long tail.

Why are geckos special?

With their broad heads and fat, stumpy tails, geckos look different from most other lizards. Most geckos have dull-colored skin that helps them to blend in with their surroundings, although some are very brightly colored. Their skin is covered with bead-like scales. These scales make some geckos feel as soft as velvet.

Geckos have some special characteristics that set them apart from other lizards. Most have toe pads that allow them to climb very well. They are also the only type of lizard that can make noises. There are laughing geckos, barking geckos, and even singing geckos! Sometimes it is hard to believe that such small creatures can make such loud noises.

In the United States, the two most common geckos are the leaf-fingered gecko and the banded, or ground, gecko. Many other species have arrived in the U.S. over the last 200 years. These species have traveled in the cargoes of ships from other countries, and have then settled down in warm areas such as Florida.

Did you know?

Geckos are very important to the world, as they eat tons of insects everyday. In some parts of the world, they are responsible for keeping down the number of household pests, such as roaches and flies.

This western banded gecko is one of the most common types of gecko found in the United States.

Protecting geckos

Many gecko species are **endangered.** There are several laws that protect endangered geckos. These laws make it illegal for people to take geckos from the wild and sell them or keep them in their homes. For this reason, the geckos that are sold in pet stores are not caught in the wild, but are born in **captivity.**

Unfortunately, the main reason that geckos are disappearing is because their habitats are being destroyed. This is a big problem throughout the world as forests are cut down to create farmland, and deserts are developed so people can live there.

7

Gecko features

Geckos are usually small creatures—the smallest are less than one inch long (2.5 cm). But they can be as big as the Tokay gecko, which measures fourteen inches (36 cm). Most geckos are **nocturnal,** which means they are mainly active at night, but a few species are **diurnal.** Nocturnal geckos have cat-like eyes, with vertical **pupils,** so they can see better in the dark. Diurnal geckos usually have round pupils.

The Tokay gecko is one of the largest geckos in the world. It can be aggressive and has a painful bite!

No eyelids?

There are two major groups of geckos. One group has eyelids and the other group does not. Most geckos belong to the group with no eyelids.

Hungry hunters

Geckos have thick, sticky tongues which they use to hunt insects. When geckos see an insect, they jump forward, grab it with their tongue, and swallow it whole. Geckos can eat many insects in one sitting. Some larger geckos even eat other lizards, small shrews, or mice. Some gecko **species** lick **nectar** out of flowers or eat small amounts of fruit.

8

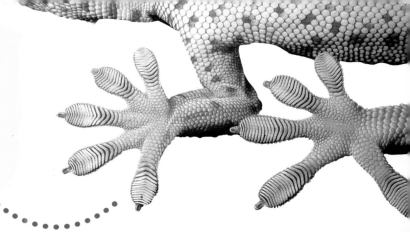

The tiny, brush-like stickers at the bottom of each toe pad increase the amount of contact that the gecko's toes have with an object. This means that a gecko can even walk on a ceiling.

Climbing high

Geckos are great climbers. At the end of each toe they have a pad covered with microscopic, brush-like stickers. The pads work like suction cups, and can stick to almost any surface the gecko climbs.

Gecko colors

Some geckos have skin colors that blend in with their surroundings. This means the gecko can **camouflage** itself to hide from hunters. Other geckos have vivid colors. They can look very pretty, like the Phelsuma gecko, which is a beautiful green and blue color.

Gecko babies

Most geckos lay eggs, but a few species give birth to live babies. Geckos lay eggs several times a year and usually lay two eggs at a time. Once she has laid her eggs, the female gecko leaves the nest for good. Fortunately, young geckos are able to look after themselves as soon as they are hatched.

The dull colors of this gecko allow it to camouflage itself against the tree trunk.

9

Geckos as pets

Lots of people keep geckos as pets. Geckos are cool and interesting—but there are so many kinds to choose from. Which one would make the best pet for you?

Texas banded geckos have velvety skin. They need to be kept in pairs.

The New Caledonian gecko eats small amounts of fruit.

The fat-tailed gecko comes from the Sahara desert. It can be quite aggressive.

The flying gecko is a large gecko that needs lots of room!

10

Which gecko?

Only a few **species** of gecko make really good pets. Some, like the Tokay gecko, should not be handled without the help of an adult because they can bite very hard. Others, like the day gecko, need special things to eat. And some need special homes because they spend a lot of time climbing.

Once you have had more experience with geckos, you might be interested in keeping a variety of species. But for the beginner, the best choice by far is the leopard gecko. Leopard geckos are one of the most interesting gecko species, and they are fun and easy to keep.

The ideal gecko

The ideal pet gecko should:
- not get too big;
- be easy to feed; and
- be gentle and not aggressive.

Young leopard geckos are striped—so they should be called "tiger geckos." But, as they get older, their stripes turn into spots.

Leopard geckos

The leopard gecko's scientific name is *Eublepharis macularius*. The first word means "good (or working) eyelids," because, unlike many geckos, leopard geckos have eyelids. The second word means "spotted." When leopard geckos are babies, the tops of their bodies are covered in stripes, which helps them to hide from **predators** by blending in with their surroundings. But as the geckos get older, their stripes shrink down to spots, so their skin looks like a leopard's skin.

11

Leopard gecko facts

Leopard geckos are small lizards that measure about six to eight inches long (20 cm). They are tan-yellow in color, with dark spots all over the top of their body. Their skin is rough and covered in growths that look like warts, but in fact these are just a kind of scale. Their bellies are plain white or tan.

Colorful geckos

Sometimes leopard geckos have different coloring. This is because **reptile breeders** have bred different types of geckos. Now you can find leopard geckos that are bright yellow, orange, or completely white.

Leopard geckos in the wild

Leopard geckos live in the rocky deserts and grasslands of southern Asia, India, Pakistan, Afghanistan, Iran, and Iraq—all areas where it gets really hot. There they spend most of the day sleeping and hiding in **crevices** in the rocks or in burrows in the sand. They keep hidden to avoid the heat of the day, but also to stay safe from birds and other animals that might eat them.

Geckos do not like sandy deserts. They prefer to hide in rocky areas during the day and come out to hunt for food at night. If the temperature of their habitat drops too low, geckos will not eat.

At night, the geckos come out of their burrows or crevices to hunt. They slither along the ground in search of food or sit and wait until a small insect comes by. Then they jump forward and catch it with their mouth. In the wild, leopard geckos eat a variety of insects, as well as scorpions! They also eat other small lizards.

Leopard geckos are different

Leopard geckos are one of the most interesting **species** of geckos. Unlike most other geckos:

- they often do not make noise;
- they have eyelids; and
- they do not have suction pads on the ends of their toes, which means there is a smaller chance they will escape!

Leopard geckos belong to a small group of geckos that have eyelids. This means they can close their eyes when they sleep.

Leopard geckos do not have sticky pads on their toes like most geckos. Their toes are pointed and more like those of other lizards.

Eggs and Babies

By the time most leopard geckos are two years old, they are old enough to **breed.** In the wild, one male leopard gecko lives close to several females. The breeding season starts when the days become shorter and the nights become cooler.

Mating

When a male leopard gecko is ready to mate, he shows off to a female by vibrating his tail. If the female decides that the male is good enough, she will let him bite her on the neck. Then they mate. After four to six weeks, the female starts to look pregnant. She becomes bigger, and pale bulges appear on her belly.

Hot or cold?

The temperature of the nest where a gecko lays her eggs makes a difference in the sex of her babies. If the nest is in a really hot area, male baby geckos are born. If the nest is in a cooler area, most of the babies will be females.

The sex of the geckos in these eggs will depend on the temperature of the nest they have been laid in.

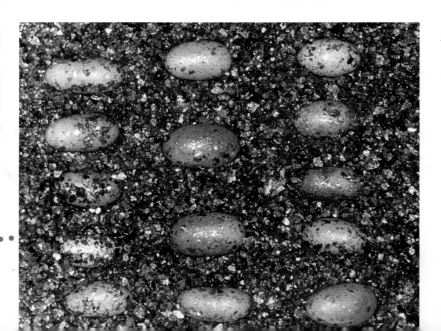

Laying eggs

When she is about six weeks pregnant, the female gecko starts to look for a warm, moist place to lay her eggs. In the wild, females dig burrows where they lay their eggs. Leopard geckos usually lay one or two eggs at a time, and a single female may lay eggs up to six times in one season. Leopard gecko eggs take around six to eight weeks to hatch.

This baby leopard gecko has only just hatched.

Baby leopard geckos

Baby leopard geckos only measure about three inches in length (8 cm), about the length of your longest finger. Once the baby geckos hatch, they are able to run as well as an adult. They need to run fast because they can easily become a **predator's** meal if they are not careful! For the first week they do not eat anything, but after that they become skillful hunters.

This young gecko is just beginning to develop its adult spots.

15

Is a Gecko for You?

Leopard geckos were one of the first lizards to be bred in **captivity** in large numbers. Now they are so popular that thousands are bred every year. Leopard geckos can make great pets, but before you buy one, you should think about some of the good and not-so-good things about keeping geckos.

Leopard gecko good points

- Leopard geckos can be found in many pet stores, so they are much easier to buy than most other **species**.
- They are not expensive.
- They are small, so they do not take up much space.
- Leopard geckos are gentle and do not bite like some other types of geckos.
- They are fun to watch because of their cat-like hunting behavior.
- They are naturally clean; they will use only one corner of their tank as a toilet.
- They can live for ten to twenty years.

Leopard geckos are tiny. Even when they are full grown, they are still small enough to hold in your hand.

Leopard gecko not-so-good points

- Leopard geckos are fragile and need gentle handling.
- They need a constant source of warmth, such as a heat lamp.
- They need to be fed live animals, like crickets, mealworms, and other insects.
- If they escape, they can hide anywhere and be very difficult to catch.
- They are **nocturnal,** so you cannot expect them to be very active during the day.
- If you keep males and females together, they **breed** easily— you may get more geckos than you bargained for!
- If you accidentally put male geckos together, they may fight.

Leopard geckos are easy to feed. But you must be comfortable handling crickets and mealworms, as these are the leopard gecko's favorite food.

Yes or no?

Having a gecko for a pet means:
- giving it food and water daily;
- cleaning out its tank once every two weeks; and
- making sure it is warm, happy, and healthy.

Are you really sure that you are prepared to do all these things, even when you are in a hurry or want to do something else? If the answer is yes, then perhaps you have just made the decision to own a gecko.

17

Buying your gecko

Geckos are often sold in pet stores, but you can also buy your gecko from a **reptile breeder.** Reptile breeders advertise in newspapers, on the Internet, and in reptile magazines. They usually have lots of useful information and can give you advice on setting up your gecko's home. They can also help you make plans for getting food for your gecko. Most reptile breeders work with a specific **species,** so you should be able to find a breeder who specializes in leopard geckos.

What to look for

At the pet store or the reptile breeder's, look at all the geckos, but make sure that the one you take home:

- is young;
- looks lively and alert;
- does not look tired or sleepy; and
- is active and runs around easily.

Top tip

Ask the pet store assistant to put some crickets or mealworms in the geckos' tank. If the gecko you like runs over and catches an insect right away–you have a winner! If your gecko does not seem interested, choose a different one.

This gecko is alert and waiting to pounce on the cricket. It would be a good choice for a pet.

How many geckos?

In the wild, leopard geckos live in **colonies.** These are loose groups that are usually made up of one male and about five females. You may decide that you want to keep two or more geckos together. However, there are some important points to remember about keeping groups of geckos.

Male geckos should not be kept together. They will fight and hurt each other. If you want to keep more than one gecko, it is best to keep females. Ask an experienced gecko keeper to show you how to recognize the females.

If you are keeping several geckos, try to choose ones that are about the same size. Otherwise, the larger ones might pick on the smaller ones, or keep them from eating.

If your parents or guardians are experienced gecko owners, they may decide that you can keep one male with several females. But if you keep a male with females, they will probably **breed.** Taking care of eggs and newly-hatched baby geckos is a big task.

It is probably best to start with one gecko. When you are comfortable with your new pet, you can think about getting a second gecko.

Your Gecko's Home

Pet geckos should be kept in glass tanks, like the ones used for fish. But even though leopard geckos are not great climbers, your tank should still have a lid to cover it, especially if you have a cat or dog. A 10-gallon (40-liter) tank will be big enough for one to three geckos. If you have more than four geckos, you will need a 15-gallon (50-liter) tank or bigger.

Your lid should snap into place over the top of the tank so your gecko cannot squeeze between the cracks and get out!

Inside the tank

Your gecko will be much more comfortable if you put a few things inside its tank. First of all, you will need some material, known as **substrate,** to line the bottom of the tank and prevent your gecko from lying on the cold glass. The gecko will use this material to lie in and crawl around in. Many things can be used for substrate, but some commonly used natural materials are medium-sized rocks, gravel, or bark. Do not use anything wet—leopard geckos are from dry **environments.** Also avoid anything that the gecko can swallow, such as sand.

If you use natural materials, they will have to be cleaned often. Artificial materials such as artificial grass, paper towels, and newspaper are easier to clean or replace, but they do not look as natural. Paper pulp substrate is sold in pet stores and makes a good material for geckos.

Food and water

Geckos need to be given live insects to eat and fresh water to drink everyday. Young geckos that are learning to hunt will eat much better if the insects are placed in a feeding bowl where the geckos can see them, but from which they cannot escape.

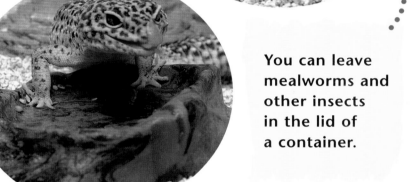

The water dish should be shallow, like the lid of a glass jar, so your gecko can easily climb in. Do not expect your gecko to drink from a dish all the time—geckos also like to lick water off plants or logs.

You can leave mealworms and other insects in the lid of a container.

Your gecko will use its tongue to lap up water.

Shelter

It is very important to give your pet a place to rest. Your gecko will be happy with a small plastic "house" or a pile of natural objects such as branches and rocks.

Making a "house" for your gecko is an easy project. Ask an adult to cut a small hole in the side of a plastic container. Put some peat moss or **vermiculite** mixture inside the house to make it moist and cozy.

21

Home comforts

Just as you need a sofa and some chairs in your house, your gecko will find its home more comfortable and interesting if you add some extra things to it. Rocks, branches, and bark will imitate the gecko's **environment** in the wild, and provide good places for your pet to climb, sleep, and find shelter.

Adding plants

There's nothing like a plant to make a house seem more like a home! Snake plants (*Sansevieria trifasciata*) and fig plants (*Ficus lyrata*) are pretty and have tough leaves that will stand up to the trampling your gecko might do.

Safety first

Always ask an experienced gecko owner which plants are safe; some plants are poisonous to geckos.

Be careful not to stack too many rocks on top of each other, as they can fall on your gecko and hurt it.

Ultraviolet light

Ultraviolet light comes from the Sun, and a lot of **reptiles** rely on it for their health. But leopard geckos are nocturnal, so they do not need an ultraviolet light source to stay healthy.

Keeping warm

Geckos come from hot areas of the world and need to stay warm, so your gecko's tank will need a **heat source.** It is best to use either a ceramic bulb, or a low-level red light bulb to supply heat. Remember that leopard geckos are **nocturnal**, so they will not like bright lights.

The daytime temperature in your gecko's tank should be between 75 and 90°F (24 and 32°C). At night this should be reduced by two or three degrees. Geckos like to move between different temperatures, so make sure it is warm at one end of the tank and cooler at the other. Ask an adult to help you set up the heat source and teach you how to use a thermometer.

This tank is heated using a low-level red light bulb. The temperature close to the bulb will be about 7°F (4°C) higher than the temperature at the other end of the tank.

Safety first

Do not use heaters that look like artificial rocks. Although some people recommend these "hot rocks" as a heat source, they are not a good idea–your gecko can burn itself on them!

Feeding Your Gecko

Geckos are fun to feed. After you have fed your gecko for a couple of weeks, it will learn when it is dinnertime. It will come out of its box to meet you when it hears you getting dinner ready, and it might even learn to eat from your hand.

With a little patience, you can teach your gecko to take food from your hand. If they can see an insect moving, leopard geckos are so curious that they are likely to come over and investigate!

Mealtimes

Because geckos are **nocturnal,** they should be fed in the evening, or just before you go to bed. Your gecko should eat once a day. But if it is a young, growing animal, it should have two small meals: one in the morning and one in the evening.

What food?

You will need a constant supply of insects for your gecko. The most common insects to feed geckos are black or brown crickets, waxmoth **larvae,** locusts, and mealworms. You can buy these insects from a pet store, or order them directly through a company that specializes in breeding insects for feeding **reptiles.** An adult gecko should eat approximately two to five crickets a day, depending on the size of the crickets.

You can watch your gecko feeding if you stay very still and quiet.

Keeping track

When you feed your gecko, watch to see how many insects it eats.

- Give it as much food as it will eat.
- Take out any insects your gecko does not eat.
- Write down how many insects you offered, and how many your gecko ate. You will soon know exactly how many insects your gecko will eat at once.

The cricket home should have holes so the crickets can breathe. But make sure that your crickets cannot get out or you will find them jumping and chirping all over your home!

Homes for food

You will need a place where your crickets and other insects can live. You can use a small tank with a lid, or a plastic container with a tight lid and small holes to allow the insects to breathe.

Feeding the food

The crickets, mealworms, waxmoth **larvae,** and locusts that you buy to feed to your gecko will need food too! Feed them a good quality insect food, available at pet stores. They will also need a clean source of water every few days. You can shred some carrot, spinach, zucchini, or other vegetables and put them in your insect tub too. Insects love fresh vegetables.

A clean, soaked sponge on a plastic plate is the best way to give your crickets water.

In a pet store, crickets are not fed, so feed them a big meal before you give them to your gecko. That way, you will give your gecko a better meal.

A varied diet

In the wild, geckos eat many different **species** of insects. So, it is a good idea to give your gecko a variety of food sources. It is also fine to feed your gecko different insects at the same time.

Safety first

Reptile vitamin powder is not intended for humans. Never eat the vitamin powder yourself.

Vitamins and calcium

Crickets, mealworms, and other insects do not have all the vitamins and minerals your gecko needs. In order to grow strong, geckos also need a complete **reptile vitamin** powder and some reptile calcium powder. You can buy both of these at a pet store. Do not feed the powders directly to your gecko—instead, sprinkle them onto the insects before you feed them to your pet.

Vacation care

When you go away on vacation, you must:

- ask a friend or neighbor to come in everyday to give your gecko water and food and check that it is warm enough;
- ask your friend to look after the insects that you feed to your gecko;
- choose someone who knows and likes your gecko and who you can trust to look after your pet;
- leave instructions about how much food to give, when to feed your pet, and how to check the temperature in its tank; and
- leave your vet's phone number in case there is an emergency.

It is hard to make a gecko eat a vitamin tablet, so sprinkle vitamin powder and calcium powder onto the crickets or mealworms just before feeding them to your gecko.

27

Caring for Your Gecko

Having a pet can be a big responsibility. If you have a gecko, you will need to do some things for it regularly.

Misting

Sometimes you will see your gecko drinking from its water dish. But to encourage your gecko to drink, you should mist it lightly with water, using a small spray bottle. Fill the bottle with clean, warm water and lightly spray your gecko every day. In the wild, geckos drink water off leaves when they feel the rain running down their bodies. Spraying your gecko encourages it to drink. It also helps the gecko to shed its skin.

Top tips

- Make sure the bottle you use to mist your gecko has never contained any cleaners or chemicals.
- Do not mist your gecko with cold water—it will give your pet too much of a shock.
- Remember to change the water in the spray bottle every day.

Your gecko will enjoy being misted. While you mist it, the gecko might close its eyes lick its face, drinking the water.

Shedding skin

Like all **reptiles**, geckos need to shed their skin regularly. So do not be surprised if you come home one day and see part of your gecko's skin falling off! Geckos rub themselves against rocks or branches to get their old skin off. And sometimes, when they are finished, they eat it! You might notice that the color of your gecko's skin looks dull just before it sheds its old skin. The new skin is often shinier and brighter than the old one.

Adult geckos shed their skin between two and four times a year. It takes a few days for the skin to come off completely.

Checking your gecko

When you lift your gecko out of its tank, get a really close look and see if it looks healthy. A baby gecko should grow pretty fast. If it is shedding its skin every couple of weeks, it is probably growing at a nice pace. It is a good idea to measure and weigh your gecko every week or so—you will need a small set of scales and a measuring tape. An adult gecko will measure between four and ten inches in length and have a nice, fat tail, but not a fat body.

You don't need to pick up your gecko to measure it. Just place a ruler next to it every week to see how fast it is growing.

Keeping things clean

Your gecko's home will need to be cleaned regularly. By making sure that your gecko's tank is clean, you will help to keep your pet healthy and happy.

Geckos make it easy

Geckos will usually only use one area of their tank as a toilet. If you notice where your gecko has chosen to have its toilet, put a piece of paper towel or newspaper there. That way you can just pick up the paper, throw it away, and replace it every other day.

Cleaning the tank

To keep your gecko healthy, its whole tank should be cleaned out once every two weeks. It is a good idea to have a small, plastic container with holes where you can put your gecko while you clean its tank. Take all the contents out of the tank and clean them individually.

The tank can be cleaned with warm water and soap, or with a household cleaner that is marked on the bottle as safe for babies. Ask an adult to help you choose the right cleaner. After using a cleaner, rinse the tank with lots of water and let it dry completely before putting back the tank contents and your gecko.

Remember to replace the paper towel every other day. If you have more than one gecko, you might have to do this every day.

Changing the water

It is very important that your gecko drinks its water from a clean dish. Make sure you empty out your gecko's water dish, rinse it clean, and refill it with fresh water every day. Otherwise, your gecko may get sick.

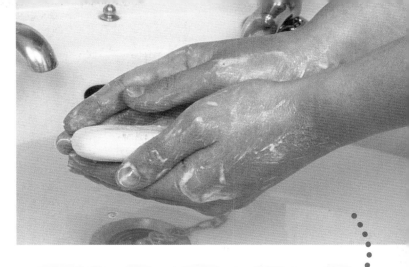

Top tip

Make a daily checklist to keep next to your gecko's tank.

Make sure you always wash your hands after cleaning your gecko's toilet area or tank.

- Has my gecko been fed?
- Does it have fresh, clean water to drink?
- Has it been misted with a spray bottle?
- Is its home clean?
- Is it warm enough? (Check the thermometer.)

Handling Your Gecko

Your gecko looks soft and cuddly, but imagine how big you seem to a gecko. Do not be surprised if when you try to catch it, your gecko seems frightened and runs away. This is normal. In the wild, geckos have lots of enemies—mostly larger animals and birds—trying to eat them. Their main defense is to run away as fast as they can and hide. Your gecko will need to get used to the idea that your hand is not something that might eat it or hurt it.

With a little patience, you can train your gecko to get used to your hand in its tank. Do not make loud noises or move very suddenly.

Picking up your gecko

When your gecko is used to your hand in its tank, you can slowly start to touch your pet.

- First, try just stroking your gecko with one finger. When it seems used to that, try picking it up slowly.
- The best way to pick up a gecko is to gently scoop it up. Place one hand above the gecko. Then close your fingers around it gently, placing your other hand underneath it at the same time.

Be careful when picking up your gecko. The tiny claws on its toes might get stuck on rocks or plants, so gently ease them off.

Tail alert!

Never pick up your gecko by its tail! When a **predator** tries to grab a gecko by the tail in the wild, the gecko's normal defense is simply to leave its tail behind! That way the gecko can make a fast getaway and the predator only gets a part of the gecko's tail. But if, by accident, the tail comes off while you are handling your gecko, do not panic—just leave the tail in the tank. In a few weeks, your gecko will have grown a brand new tail. It may be a different color and it is likely to be shorter than the original tail.

Do not worry if your gecko loses its tail by accident. Luckily, geckos can grow new tails.

Tail facts

Although your gecko can shed its tail and still survive, tails are very important for geckos.

- They use their tail for balance.
- They store fat in their tail. If they shed their tail, geckos have to eat more to regain all the weight they have lost.

33

Handle with care

When you are holding your pet, do not be surprised if it wiggles. It might even wiggle out of your hands and run off. It is better if you hold your gecko over a table or bed so it does not fall to the ground. If it gets away, it will probably run and hide. Ask an adult to help you find your gecko and return it to its tank as soon as possible. If it gets covered in dust during its adventure, get rid of the dust by gently washing your gecko in a shallow bath of warm water or by misting it with your spray bottle.

You can turn off the lights in the room and use a low-level red light or a low-power flashlight to watch your leopard gecko hunt and move about. Remember, its day starts after your bedtime.

Gecko watching

One of the best ways to enjoy your gecko is to sit and watch it while it is safe in its tank. Feeding time is always fun and if you have more than one gecko, watching how they behave together is great. So, pull up a chair and observe what your gecko does in the evening.

Geckos are good hunters. When you put an insect in their tank, they will move their head to follow the insect and run after it quickly.

Safety first

Even a healthy, clean gecko can have **bacteria** on its body that could make you sick. To avoid picking up these germs, you should always remember the following:

- Wash your hands with warm water and soap each time you finish handling your gecko.
- Do not eat while you are playing with your gecko.
- Do not let your gecko run across places where you put food, such as kitchen counters.

Common Problems

Although leopard geckos are really easy to take care of, your gecko might have some problems. If you notice anything wrong, tell an adult and write it down. Then try asking yourself the following questions:

- When was the last time your gecko was fed?
- When was the last time it ate normally?
- When did you last see your gecko drinking?
- When did it last shed its skin normally?
- When was the last time your gecko looked normal?

These questions will help you to work out how long your gecko has been sick.

No energy

If your gecko is not as active as usual, there may be a temperature problem. When geckos get cold, they do not have the energy to move around normally. Check the thermometer in your gecko's tank to make sure that it is warm enough. If the temperature is below 75°F (24°C), ask an adult to help you adjust the **heat source.** Maybe the heat bulb is broken and your gecko has become cold.

If you have to take your gecko to the vet, it will be very helpful to remember all the details about when your pet became sick.

When geckos get cold, they are less active than normal and may look sleepy.

Shedding problems

You might notice that your gecko is not shedding its skin properly. For example, if parts of its old skin stay stuck to its body for more than a couple of days, gently soak it in a warm water bath. Make sure it has a rock or a branch in its tank that it can rub against to help remove the old skin. If there is still skin hanging onto parts of your gecko's body, take your pet to a veterinarian.

Happy and healthy?

If the answer to all these questions is "yes," then you are probably taking good care of your gecko:

- Is your gecko eating?
- Is your gecko drinking?
- Is your gecko's home clean?
- Does your gecko look healthy?
- Is your gecko shedding its skin normally?
- Is your baby gecko growing normally?

Sometimes a warm bath can moisten your gecko's skin and help it to finish shedding normally.

37

Eating problems

There are many reasons why your gecko might not eat. It may be because the gecko is too cold, because it is ill, or because it does not like the food you are offering. If you notice that your gecko is not eating its crickets like it used to, pick it up gently and check it carefully. Sometimes geckos get tired of eating the same thing all the time. Try feeding it a different kind of insect, but also tell an adult what is happening.

If the problem continues...

If your gecko is still not eating after you have changed its diet, and if it seems less active than usual even when the temperature is warm enough, then it may be sick. This is especially likely if your gecko does not respond to your hand or touch like it used to, if its skin looks saggy and wrinkly, or if it keeps its eyes closed a lot. Tell an adult immediately and talk to them about making an appointment with a vet to have your pet examined.

If you are worried about your gecko, talk to an adult about taking it to a vet. Many gecko diseases can be treated by a vet.

Don't forget

Most **reptiles** can survive for days or even weeks without eating. But they cannot live without water. Make sure your gecko has clean, fresh water every day. You can encourage your gecko to drink by misting it gently with the spray bottle, or by soaking it in a shallow bath of warm water for a few minutes.

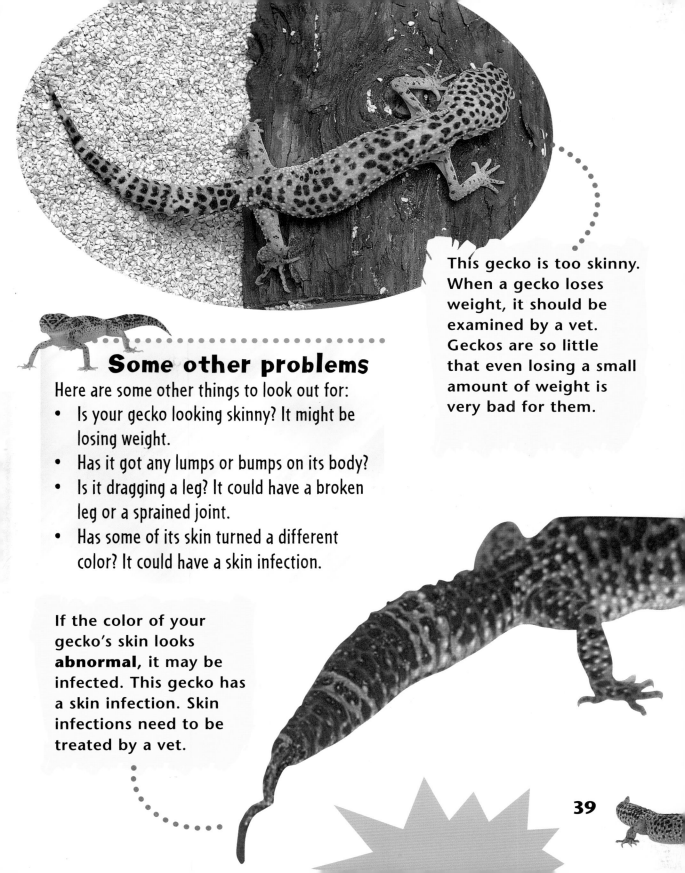

This gecko is too skinny. When a gecko loses weight, it should be examined by a vet. Geckos are so little that even losing a small amount of weight is very bad for them.

Some other problems

Here are some other things to look out for:

- Is your gecko looking skinny? It might be losing weight.
- Has it got any lumps or bumps on its body?
- Is it dragging a leg? It could have a broken leg or a sprained joint.
- Has some of its skin turned a different color? It could have a skin infection.

If the color of your gecko's skin looks **abnormal**, it may be infected. This gecko has a skin infection. Skin infections need to be treated by a vet.

Visiting the Vet

Your new gecko will need to visit a vet regularly for a physical examination. But your gecko will not need any shots unless it is sick. Soon after you buy your gecko, ask an adult to make an appointment with a vet who is used to working with **reptiles.** This will give your vet a chance to meet your gecko. The vet can also give you advice on how to care for your pet and how to recognize when it might be ill.

Checking your pet

Your vet will want to give your gecko a thorough physical examination. During the examination the vet will probably:

- weigh your gecko;
- watch your gecko from a distance to make sure it is active and lively;
- look for **mites** and other skin **parasites;**
- make sure the gecko is not too skinny;
- open its mouth and look at its teeth and gums;
- feel the gecko's belly to make sure the **organs** inside are normal;
- check its legs;
- listen to its heart and lungs; and
- check a sample of your gecko's droppings to make sure they do not contain parasites.

Your vet will examine your gecko carefully to make sure it was not ill when you bought it.

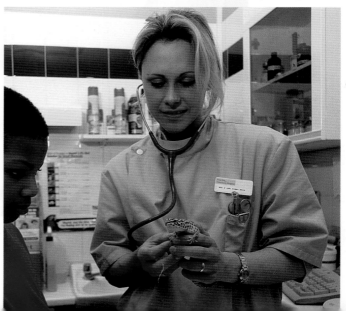

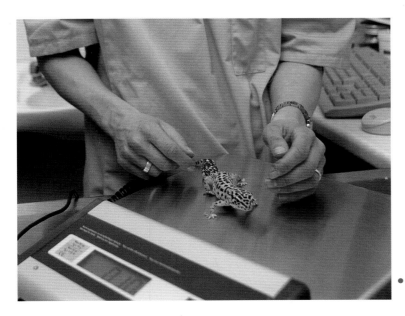

Ask your vet to tell you how much your gecko weighs and write it down, along with the date. This will be useful when you weigh your pet at home, so you can tell if it is gaining or losing weight.

Saying goodbye

Leopard geckos can live for as long as twenty years, but no matter how well you care for your pet, one day it will die. Sometimes a gecko will die peacefully and unexpectedly at home. This will come as a shock to you, but do not blame yourself. There is probably nothing you could have done.

As a caring owner, the hardest responsibility of all is to know when to let your pet be put to sleep to save it from suffering. Your gecko may be very old and in pain. Or it may have a serious illness that cannot be cured. Your vet will give your gecko a small shot. This does not hurt your pet—it just makes it sleepy. Before you can count to ten, your gecko will be asleep for the last time.

Feeling upset

However it happens, you will feel upset when your gecko dies, especially if it has been a friend for many years. It is perfectly normal for people—adults as well as children—to be sad when a pet dies, or when they think of a dead pet.

41

Keeping a Record

Owning a leopard gecko can be a big responsibility. It is difficult to remember all the important things you need to do in order to keep your gecko healthy and happy. Making a gecko scrapbook is a good way to keep all the information handy for when you need it.

Filling your scrapbook

There are many things you can write in your scrapbook. You can start by describing your trip to the pet store or to the **reptile breeder.** You may also want to describe the first day you brought your gecko home so you can look back later and remember how you felt and what your gecko looked like!

Write down the name you chose for your gecko. Also make a note of how much your gecko weighed and how long it was when you brought it home.

When you take your gecko to the vet for its first visit, write down what happens there. Keep important details, like the name and phone number of your vet, in your scrapbook.

Your scrapbook will contain important information about your gecko and how to care for your pet. It will also be a place to put pictures of your pet.

Important information

Write down information about your pet in your scrapbook:

- When you start to feed your gecko, keep a note of how much it eats.
- Each time you weigh and measure your gecko, write down its weight and length.
- Whenever your gecko does something unusual, write it down.
- Stick labels from **vitamin** powder, cricket food, and other things you need into your scrapbook.

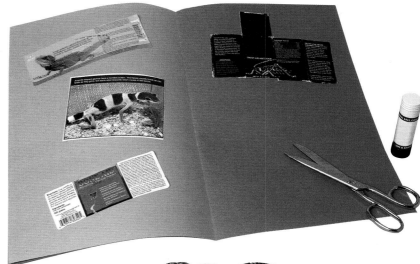

Top tip

Collect magazine articles on leopard geckos and other geckos, cut them out, and stick them in your scrapbook.

Soon you will have a complete gecko record. When you take your gecko to the vet for check-ups or if it is ill, bring your scrapbook. The information may be very useful.

Finding Out More

Geckos are very popular pets. Lots of people love geckos because they look so interesting and behave in such fascinating ways. But keeping a gecko of your own will make you appreciate geckos even more. Once you have a gecko as a pet, you will want to find out more about geckos and their lives.

Reading books and magazines about geckos and other **reptiles** will help you to understand more about your pet.

Sharing the fun

Many people throughout the world keep geckos. It is fun and helpful to get in touch with other people who love geckos as much as you do. In fact, if you ask around at school, you may find other kids like you who keep geckos as pets! Bring some pictures of your gecko to school. Draw your gecko's home or take a photo of it to show to your science teacher.

Getting together with other kids who appreciate geckos can be fun. They can tell you about their experiences with their geckos and you can share your stories, too.

Now try this

Here are some more ways to find out about geckos:

- Check out your local library and bookstore—there are hundreds of books about geckos and many of these have very helpful information on keeping leopard geckos.
- Visit zoos and nature centers—they will have fascinating reptiles to watch and lots of information on reptiles in the wild.
- With an adult, visit gecko lovers' websites, or the websites of reptile **breeders.** There you will see beautiful pictures of many types of geckos and read about their unusual lives.
- Find out about magazines on reptiles or geckos. Perhaps you will be able to subscribe to one of these magazines.
- Ask an adult to help you find a local **herpetology** group. Herpetology means the study of reptiles and amphibians. Amphibians are animals like frogs and toads.
- Get in touch with a reptile breeder—your local breeder will probably know of other kids that are interested in geckos. You can talk to them, and maybe start a leopard gecko fan club!

Most zoos have a reptile house with a wide range of reptiles of different sizes.

Glossary

abnormal different from what is usual or normal

arboreal related to, or living in, trees

bacteria tiny one-celled creatures that can cause disease

bask lie in the Sun and absorb its warmth

breed mate and then give birth to young

breeder someone who keeps animals and encourages them to mate and produce young

camouflage colors and markings that blend in with the surroundings

captivity under the control of humans

cold-blooded having the same body temperature as the surrounding air or water

colony group of creatures that live together

crevice narrow crack

diurnal active during the day

endangered at risk of being completely wiped out

environment surroundings and weather conditions in an area

habitat place where an animal or plant lives and grows

heat source place where warmth or heat comes from, such as the Sun

herpetology study of reptiles and amphibians

larva (plural larvae) young of an insect when it has just come out of an egg and looks like a worm

mite small, blood-sucking insect

nectar sweet, sugary liquid inside a flower

nocturnal active at night

organ part of the body that has a specific purpose, like the liver

parasite small creature, such as a tick or worm, that lives on or in another animal's body

predator animal that lives by killing or eating other animals

pupil dark hole in the middle of the colored part of an eye

reptile cold-blooded animal with scaly or tough skin

species group of animals that is similar

substrate soft material put in the bottom of an animal tank

ultraviolet light with wavelengths shorter than the human eye can see

vermiculite yellow or brown mineral, a bit like soil, used to line the bottom of pet tanks

vitamin important substance found in food that helps people and animals to stay healthy

Further Reading

Bartlett, Richard D. and Patricia Pope. *Day Geckos.* Hauppauge, N.Y.:
    Barron's Educational Series, Incorporated, 2001.

Pavia, Audrey. *The Gecko: An Owner's Guide to a Happy Healthy Pet.*
    New York: John Wiley & Sons, Incorporated, 1998.

Stoops, Erik Daniel. *Geckos and Their Relatives.* Benton Harbor, Mich.:
    Faulkner's Publishing Group, 1997.

Walls, Jerry G. and Maleta. *Geckos.* Neptune, N.J.: T.F.H.
    Publications, Incorporated, 1997.

Useful Addresses

Global Gecko Association
4920 Chester St.
Spencer, OK 73084-2560
http://www.gekkota.com/

The Center for North American Herpetology
http://www.naherpetology.org/

The American Society for the Prevention of Cruelty to Animals
424 E. 92nd St.
New York, NY 10128
Tel: (212) 876-7700
http://www.aspca.org

National Alternative Pet Association
P.O. Box 369
Burnet, TX 78611
http://www.altpet.net/

Disclaimer
All Internet addresses (URLs) given in this book were valid at the time of going to
press. However, due to the dynamic nature of the Internet, some addresses may have
changed, or sites may have ceased to exist since publication. While the author and
publisher regret any inconvenience this may cause readers, no responsibility for any
such changes can be accepted by either the author or the publisher.

Index